Francis Marion Crawford

Bar Harbor

Francis Marion Crawford

Bar Harbor

ISBN/EAN: 9783744727389

Printed in Europe, USA, Canada, Australia, Japan

Cover: Foto ©ninafisch / pixelio.de

More available books at **www.hansebooks.com**

Bar Harbor

*American
Summer
Resorts*

The North Shore. By ROBERT
GRANT.
With Illustrations by W. T. SMED-
LEY.

Newport. By W. C. BROWNELL.
With Illustrations by W. S. VAN-
DERBILT ALLEN.

Bar Harbor. By F. MARION CRAW-
FORD.
With Illustrations by C. S. REIN-
HART.

Lenox. By GEORGE A. HIBBARD.
With Illustrations by W. S. VAN-
DERBILT ALLEN.

** Each 12mo. Cloth. Price, 75 cents

Canoeing

BAR HARBOR

BY

F. MARION CRAWFORD

ILLUSTRATED BY

C. S. REINHART

LIST OF ILLUSTRATIONS

THE first impression made by Bar Harbor at the height of its season upon the mind of one fresh from a more staid and crystallized civilization is that it is passing through a period of transition, in which there is some of the awkwardness which we associate with rapid growth, and something also of the youthful freshness which gives that very awkwardness a charm. The name of Mount Desert suggests, perhaps, a grim and forbidding cliff, frowning upon the pale waves of a melancholy ocean. Instead, the traveller who crosses the bay in the level light of an August afternoon looks upon the soft, rolling outline of wooded hills, on the highest of which a little hotel breaks the sky-line, upon a shore along which villas and cottages stretch on either side of a toy wooden village, which looks as though it were to be put away in a box at night, and upon the surrounding sea, an almost land-locked inlet, in which other islands, like satellites of Mount Desert, are scattered here and there.

As the little steamer draws up to her moorings the groups of people waiting on the pier stand out distinctly, and the usual types detach themselves one by one. The clusters of hotel-runners and express-men are lounging listlessly until they shall be roused to clamorous activity by the landing of the first passenger; in knots

2

and pairs, those serenely idle people of all ages, who, in all places and seasons, seem to find an ever-new amusement in watching the arrival of trains or boats, are as deeply interested as usual ; the inevitable big and solemn dog, of nondescript breed and eclectic affections, is stalking about with an air of responsibility.

And yet the little crowd is not quite like other gatherings on other piers. Girls in smart cotton frocks are sitting in shining little village carts, with grooms at their horses' sleek heads, wedged in between empty buck-boards that look like paralyzed centipedes, the drivers of which wear clothes ranging from the livery of the large stables to the weather-bleached coat of the " native" from Cherryfield or Ellsworth, who has brought over his horse to take his share of the " rusticator's " ready money during the short season. There are no hotel omnibuses, no covered traps of any kind, as becomes a holiday place where winter and rough weather are enemies not meant to be reckoned with ;

3

everybody seems either to know every-one else, or not to care if he does not, and there is an air of cheerful informality about the whole scene which immediately makes one feel welcome and at home.

In order not to be behind every self-respecting town throughout the Western world Bar Harbor has a Main Street, which plunges violently down a steep place toward the pier, and which is beautified for a short distance by a mushroom growth of tents and shanties, the summer home of the almond-eyed laundryman, the itin-erant photographer with a specialty of tintypes, and the seller of weary-looking fruit, of sandwiches that have seen better days, and temperance drinks of gorgeous hues. Plymouth Rock also vaunts its "pants," and young ladies are recom-mended to grow up with Castoria.

Then come the more necessary shops— the tinsmith's, at whose door a large bull-terrier benevolently grins all day; the tailor's, where one may study the fashions of New York filtered through Bangor;

the china shop, where bright-colored lamp-shades spread themselves like great butter-flies in the window, and the establishment of Mr. Bee, the locally famous and indispensable provider of summer literature, and of appropriate alleviations for the same, in the shape of caramels, cigarettes, and chewing-gum. Directly opposite stands a huge hotel, apparently closed or almost deserted, but evidently built in the years when the gnawing tooth of the national jig-saw grievously tormented all manner of wood-work, a melancholy relic of an earlier time when, as "Rodick's," it was almost another name for Bar Harbor itself.

No lover of Bar Harbor has been found bold enough to say that Main Street is pretty; and yet, between ten and twelve o'clock on a summer's morning, it has a character, if not a beauty, of its own. Alongside of the "board walk," which takes the place of a pavement, the buckboards are drawn up, waiting to be hired; in some of them, often drawn by four horses, are parties of people, consisting usually of more women than men, as is becoming in New England, already starting upon one of the longer expeditions, and only stopping to collect a stray member or to lay in a stock of fruit and sugar-plumbs. Farmers' carts, with closed hoods like Shaker sunbonnets, are on their rounds from one cottage to another, meandering through the crowd, and driven with exasperating calmness by people who sit far back in their little tunnels, and cannot possibly see on either side of them to get out of anyone else's way. Then there are all sorts of light private traps, usually driven by women or girls bound on household errands or visits, and psychologically unbalanced between their desire to speak to the friends who meet them on foot, and their anxiety lest they should be forced to recognize the particular acquaintance on whom they are just going to call.

Along the board walk there is a row of little shops, some of them scarcely larger than booths, the proprietors of which perch like birds of passage, pluming them-

The
Landing
Stage

selves in the sunshine of the brief season, and taking flight again before the autumn gales. In one window a lot of Turkish finery looks curiously exotic, especially the little slippers, gay with tassels and embroidery, turning up their pointed toes as if scorning the stouter footgear which tramps along outside. Another shop is bright with the crude colors of Spanish scarfs and pottery; in another, Japanese wares manage to keep their faint smell of the East in spite of the salt northern air, and farther on you may wonder at the misplaced ingenuity of Florida shell jewelry, and be fascinated by the rakish leer of the varnished alligator.

By one of the contrasts which make Bar Harbor peculiarly attractive, next door to these cosmopolitan shops there still thrives one of the indigenous general stores, where salt fish are sold, and household furniture and crockery, and the candy peculiar to New England stores and New York peanut stands, which keeps through all vicissitudes a vague odor of sawdust, and where you may also buy, as was once advertised by the ingenuous dealer, "baby carriages, butter, and paint."

Should you wish to give a message to a friend without the trouble of writing a note, the chances are more than even that you will find him or her any morning on the board-walk, or in the neighborhood of the post-office, for as there is no delivery at Bar Harbor, and as the mails are often delayed, there is ample opportunity to search for an acquaintance in the waiting crowd. Here also congregate the grooms in undress livery, with leather mail-bags slung under one arm, who have ridden in from the outlying cottages, and who walk their horses up and down, or exchange stable notes with their acquaintances; sailors from private yachts, usually big, fair Scandinavians; mail orderlies from any men-of-war which may happen to be in port; boys and girls who do not find the waiting long, and all that mysterious tribe of people who look as if they could not possibly receive a dozen letters a year, and

yet who are always assiduously looking
out for them. As usual, the post-office is
a loadstone for all the dogs in the village,
and as there are many strangers among
them, of all breeds and ages and tempers,
walking round and round one another with
stiff legs and bristling backs, unregenerate
man is kept in tremulous expectation of a
dog-fight as free as any in Stamboul. But
somehow the fight rarely comes off, though
the resident canine population has become
fearfully and wonderfully mixed, through
the outsiders who have loved and ridden
away. One nondescript, especially, is not
soon forgotten, a nightmare cross of a
creature in which the curly locks and
feathery tail of the spaniel are violently
modified by the characteristic pointed
breastbone and bandy legs of a dachs-
hund.

Wandering through the streets of the
little village one is struck again and again
by the sharp contrast between what may
be called the natural life of the place and
the artificial condition which fashion has

imposed upon it. In some of the streets almost every house is evidently meant to be rented, the owners usually retiring to restricted quarters at the back, where they stow themselves away and hang themselves up on pegs until they may come into their own again. Here and there a native cottage has been bought and altered by a summer resident, and over the whole there is the peculiarly smug expression of a quarter which is accustomed to put its best foot foremost for a few months of the year. But in the back lanes and side-streets there are still the conditions of the small New England community, in which land is poor and work is slack during the long winter, so that although there is no abject poverty in the sense in which it is known to cities, there is also little time or inclination for the mere prettiness of life.

An element of the picturesque is supplied by an Indian camp, which used for years to be pitched in a marshy field known as Squaw Hollow; but with the advent of a Village Improvement Society

certain newfangled and disturbing ideas as
to sanitary conditions obtained a hearing,
and the Indians were banished to a back
road out of the way of sensitive eyes and
noses. They claim to be of the Passama-
quoddy tribe, speak their own language,
and follow the peaceful trades of basket-
weaving and moccasin-making, and the
building of birch-bark canoes. Their little dwellings—some of them tents, some
of them shanties covered with tar-paper
and strips of bark—are scattered about,
and in the shadow of one of them sits a
lady of enormous girth, who calls herself
their queen, and who wears, perhaps as a
badge of sovereignty, a huge fur cap even
in the hottest weather. She is not less
industrious than other "regular royal"
queens, for she sells baskets and tells for-
tunes even more flattering than the fabled
tale of Hope. Some of the young men
are fine, swarthy, taciturn creatures, who
look as though they knew how to put a
knife to other uses than whittling the
frame of a canoe; but one does not feel

tempted to rush upon Fate for the sake of any of the dumpy and greasy-looking damsels who will soon become like their even dumpier and greasier mothers.

The whole encampment is pungent with the acrid smoke of green wood, and many children—round, good-natured balls of fat in all shades of yellow and brown—roll about in close friendship with queer little dogs, in which the absence of breed produces a family likeness. It is curious to see in the characteristic work of these people the survival of the instinctive taste of semi-savage races, and the total lack of it in everything else. The designs cut on the bark of their canoes, the cunningly blended colors in their basket-work, are thoroughly good in their way; but contact with a higher civilization seems to have affected them as it has the Japanese, turning their attention chiefly to making napkin-rings and collar-boxes, and to a hideous delight in tawdry finery, which is fondly, though distantly, modelled on current American fashions.

16

Bar Harbor drinks the cup of summer standing. In mid-April the snow may lie six feet deep, and before the end of October long icicles are often hanging on the north side of the rocks, while even in August the northern lights shoot up their quivering, spectral spears from the horizon to the zenith. Some fierce days of heat there are in July, but on the whole the temperature is decidedly arctic, especially to one accustomed to a less rigorous climate. In New York we are used to having the kindly fruits of the earth brought to us long before their natural season, and it sounds strangely to be told at Bar Harbor that the first garden strawberries may be looked for about the fourth of July, and that June lilies will bloom early in August; but such trifles only give one a feeling of chasing the summer, as climate-fanciers follow the spring, and are certainly not to be reckoned as grievances.

The people who have a certain very slight right to complain are the artists, who, having heard of the beauties of

Mount Desert, come prepared to carry away at least a reminder of them on canvas or paper. They find that they have fallen upon a spot almost entirely deficient in what painters term "atmosphere," and of which the characteristic effects almost defy reproduction. In what is known as a "real Bar Harbor day" the air is so thin and clear that there seem to be no distant effects, and objects lose their relative values. The sea is of a darker blue than the sky, and the rocks are very red or very gray, and the birches are of a brighter green than the firs, which stand out against the sky with edges as sharp as those of the tightly curled trees on wooden stands in the toy Swiss farm-yards dear to our youth. But that is all. Even the clouds seem to abjure mystery and take definite outlines; the water is spangled with shining points where the light breeze ruffles it, and one can see every patch on the sail of the old fishing-schooner making her leisurely way to her anchorage. Any attempt at a faithful rendering of such dry brilliancy is apt

to have a fatal likeness to a chromo-lithograph, and the artist usually ends by leaving his paint-box at home, and giving himself up to enjoyment of the keen air that tingles through his veins like wine.

The truthful chronicler is forced to admit that the climate of Bar Harbor has two drawbacks—high wind and fog, one usually following the other. Out of a clear sky, without a cloud, while the sun grins away derisively overhead, a southwest gale will often blow a whole day, filling the village streets with stinging dust and the whirling disks of vagrant hats, and making the little fleet of catboats and launches in the harbor duck and strain at their moorings; turning venturesome girls who try to walk into struggling pillars of strangely twisted drapery, and even in the heart of the warm woods tearing at the crowded trees so that they sigh and creek as they rub their weary old limbs against one another. The second day is gray and cloudy, on the third it rains, but still the wind blows, a nervous wind that makes one long to pick a quarrel with one's best friend. And then the wind drops as suddenly as it rose, and the next day all discomfort, past and to come, is forgotten for awhile in sheer delight of beauty. For the air is still, and the sun shines gently on a dull green sea over which little shivers run now and then, and far in the offing there is the gray line of a fog-bank. Slowly it comes in with the southeast wind, stealing along the surface of the water, now closing softly round an island, then rising from it like a wreath of smoke, here piled into a fleecy mass, there turned to silver and scattered by a sunbeam, but coming on and on, and creeping up and up, until the trees on the Porcupines have their feet in the clouds like Wagnerian heroes; and presently they also are hidden, and the whole harbor is swathed in a soft cloud, from the depths of which come now and then the muffled, anxious whistles of the little steamers which ply about the bay—the Silver Star, from Winter Harbor; the Cimbria, from Bangor; and louder and deeper, the hoarse note of the Sappho as she feels her way across with passengers from the ferry.

When the oldest inhabitant is asked how long a fog may last he will shake his head, shift his quid, and decline to commit himself. There is a legend of a young man who came in on a yacht some years ago, duly prepared to enjoy himself and admire the scenery. His skipper groped his way to an anchorage in a mist so dense that he could not see fifty feet ahead or astern ; the luckless young man went about for nine mortal days, swathed in a soft, smothering blanket ; on the tenth day he sailed away, still in a thick fog, and swear-in mighty oaths. Even when the fog lies over the bay the air may be quite clear in-land, and after a drive among the hills it is a curious sensation to come back to the shore. In the wooded uplands all is sunny and cheerful, but when the village is reached a cold breath is stealing through it as though the door of an ice-house had been left open, and on turning down a

side-street toward the sea a gray wall of
mist blots out trees and shore alike.

To anyone not familiar with it, catboat
sailing in a thick fog does not suggest itself
as an amusement. It has a strong attrac-
tion of its own, however, for the breeze is
usually steady, and the entire obliteration
of the familiar landmarks gives an element
of uncertainty and adventure. The course
must be steered by the compass, and it is
necessary to have accurate notes of the
local bearings. If the harbor is at all
crowded the little boat feels her way out
slowly, close-hauled, as carefully as though
she were alive ; but once in the freer water
the sheet is started, and she slips forward
into infinite mystery. Every sense is
strained to take the place of sight, which
is baffled and almost useless in the thickly
pressing veil that now and then grows
thinner for a moment, only to close in
again more densely. The sharp lapping of
the water against the sides of the boat, the
wash of the rising tide upon some island,
the shrill scream of a gull overhead, the

whistle of a launch astern in the harbor—
all these make to themselves echoes, and
by and by the far-off beat of a side-wheel
steamer throbs with a great palpitation in
the stillness.   Boats which ply for profit
or sail for pleasure are apt to make noise
enough in a fog ; but the fishermen give
themselves less trouble, and slipping along,
ghost-like, one may be suddenly aware of
a larger and darker phantom ahead, to
which it is wise to give a respectfully wide
birth, without insisting too much upon the
privileges of the starboard tack and the
possible right of way, when the water is
over-cold for much swimming.   There
does not seem to be any particular reason
for ever turning back, when one is not
bound for any visible point, and you may
dream your dream out before you come
about and run free for the harbor again.
The fog is, if anything, thicker than when
you started, and it is no easy matter to
find your berth ; but the boat seems to
" kinder smell her way," as an old sailor
once remarked in a like case, and at last

she bumps gently against her mooring-buoy.

The most beautiful effects of fog at Bar Harbor are to be seen from Newport Mountain, which is about a thousand feet high, and is a mile or two out of the village. At first the path leads upward among thick woods, through which the sunlight falls in yellow patches, and where the squirrels chatter angrily from the spruce boughs. This part of the way is very pretty, though it is apt to be warm, and in early summer the black flies make succulent meals on the nape of the pilgrim's neck. A little farther on, the path leads out over broad open stretches of granite rock, scratched and furrowed by a primeval glacier, with scrubby tufts of mountain laurel growing in the stony hollows, and blueberry bushes holding on for dear life everywhere. Oddly enough, it is the easiest thing in the world to lose the path, although it has been considerately marked with a line of small cairns, which, however, are set at varying distances

apart, often as far as a couple of hundred
feet each from the next, and are built up
of fragments of the rock itself, so that they
are hard to distinguish in a failing light.
To miss the path means wandering aim-
lessly over the slippery rock-slopes, or
striking down the hill-side through the
almost impenetrable underbrush, with the
further penalty, especially if one happen
to have a companion of the other sex, of
being unmercifully jeered at; for to have
lost one's way on Newport Mountain is
as well-worn an excuse at Bar Harbor as
it is, in town, to say that one's cab did not
come.

Once fairly at the top, and having con-
scientiously looked at the view all round,
there is no lack of sheltered corners for
smoke and contemplation.   On the one
hand the open sea stretches out, a sheet of
gray steel, with great patches of speckled
froth and foam here and there, near the
shore, like white leopard skins, flung off
by the grim puritan rocks that will have
none of such heathenish adorning.   On

the other hand the mainland stretches its cruel, jagged line beyond Schoodie, and the lighthouse on Egg Rock stands up straight as a sentinel to guard the bay. Two or three big men-of-war lying in the harbor might be taken for neat models, of themselves, and the little craft moving about them are like water-beetles or flitting white moths. But the sea has changed suddenly, and it shivers all over as though the cold water could feel yet colder, and all at once the fog-bank that has been lying so innocently outside begins to unfold itself and steal forward over the surface. There does not seem to be much air above, and the trees on the Porcupines are still free. But on the right all is very different. Through the deep gorge or cleft between Newport and Dry Mountain, into which the sun has been beating all day, the chilly fog-wind now draws hard, and the fleecy cloud pours after it. Nothing, perhaps, could be less like the stern side of Dry Mountain than the gracious sweep of Mount Ida, and yet, as one looks, the lines of Tennyson's " Œnone " rise to the memory :

> " The swimming vapor slopes athwart the glen,
> Puts forth an arm, and creeps from pine to pine,
> And loiters, slowly drawn."

But you will do well not to loiter too long yourself, for gray cairns are ill to find in a gray mist, and you had better gain the woods by the time the top of Newport is swathed in cloud as though it were a real grown-up mountain.

Mount Desert is lucky in its proper names of places, having been discovered as a summer resort late enough to escape the semi-classical namings of " Baths " and " Mirrors " and " Bowers," which have sentimentalized the rocks and pools of the White Mountains. A few French words still linger as a reminder of the time when Louis XIV. gave the original grant to the Sieur de la Motte Cadillac ; but most of them, like Hull's Cove and Town Hill, have an honest colonial American ring, while about Pretty Marsh Harbor there is a certain echo of romance, and " Junk o'

Pork" and "Rum Key," two little islands, or rather rocks, in the bay, have a very nautical, and even piratical, suggestiveness.

At the first glance the island, on a map, reminds one somewhat of the dejected lamb which hangs by his middle in the order of the Golden Fleece. The deep indentation is Somes's Sound, running far inland, with Somesville at its head, a quiet New England village, with a white meeting-house, and many other houses, most of them also white, and standing among gnarled apple-trees, in a gentle, dozing tranquillity from which the place is roused when parties drive over from Bar Harbor to eat broiled chickens and "pop-overs" at the local hotel, and to drive back by moonlight—expeditions which are considered to have sufficient local color to entitle them to notice, without omission of the popovers, in Baedeker's recent "Guide to the United States."

In the neighborhood of Somesville the characteristics of the native population are

much more noticeable than at Bar Harbor,
only eight miles away, where a watering-
place has been grafted on a fishing village.
At some time or other in his life almost
every islander seems to have followed the
sea ; the man who drives your buckboard
may have been more than once to China,
and it is extremely likely that the farmer
who brings you your green peas has been
tossed for many a week of hours in a crazy
dory off the deadly Banks, which cost us
every year so many lives. In nearly every
home there is some keepsake from far
away lands, some tribute from arctic or
tropic seas, and when at last an old captain
makes up his mind to stay ashore it is certain that there will be something about his
house to show his former calling—a pair of
huge whale-ribs on either side of the front
door, flowers growing in shells that have
held the murmur of the Indian Ocean, and,
instead of a cock or banner, a model of
some sort of boat perched on the barn for
a weather-vane. That a sailor-man is a
handy man is true the world over, but the

Maine man seems to have an especial knack with wood, from the lumber-camp to the cabinetmaker's bench, and many a carpenter working by the day will turn out a well-finished sideboard or an odd piece of artistic furniture from the roughest sort of pencil sketch. They are good smiths, too, and the best of their wrought-iron recalls the breadth and freedom of the early German and Italian work.

Society at Bar Harbor does not now differ in any particularly salient manner from good society anywhere else, except that it is rather more cosmopolitan. When the guests at a small dinner or luncheon may have come from New York, Philadelphia, Boston, Washington, and Chicago, it is impossible that the conversation should fall into that jargon of a clique which often makes the talk of the most centralized society, like that of Paris or London, seem narrow and provincial to the unfortunate outsider.

One amusing survival of the simpler early days is the habit of going out in the

evening in uncovered traps. There are a few private broughams, but if you are dining out, and happen to reach the house as a lady drives up, the chances are that you will help her to alight from an open buckboard, her smart French frock shrouded in a long cloak, and her head more or less muffled and protected. One or two of the livery-stables have hacks which must have been very old when they were brought from Bangor, and which now hold together almost by a miracle. A year or two ago one of them could never be sent out without two men on the box, not indeed for the sake of lending the turnout any fictitious splendor, but because one of them had to "mind the door," which was broken, and could neither be shut nor opened by any one inside. If two or three entertainments take place on the same night there is telephoning loud and long for these antediluvian vehicles, as the only other alternative is to take a sort of carry-all with leather side-curtains which have a treacherous way of blowing open

37

and dropping small waterspouts down the back of one's neck.

It would be out of place for a mere visitor to launch into predictions regarding the social future of Bar Harbor. But one thing at least seems certain—it can never be in any sense a rival to Newport. The conditions which make the summer life of the latter more brilliant than that of any other watering-place in the world, mark it also as the playground of a great commercial metropolis, and a large proportion of its pleasure-seekers would not dare to be eighteen hours distant from New York, as they must be at Bar Harbor, until our means of getting about shall be singularly improved.

Then there are not the opportunities for display of riches and for social competition which already exist at Newport. The villas and cottages are scattered and isolated; there is no convenient central point of general meeting, and the roads are too hilly for any but light American carriages. Some victorias manage to trundle about, but the horses which draw them, or hold back their weight, look far from comfortable, and although occasional coaches have made a brief appearance they have not been a success, as on most of the thickly wooded roads their passengers are in danger of the fate of Absalom. There is an Ocean Drive which is fine in parts, and another road runs above the upper bay, seeming in some places to overhang the water, and affording a charming view of the Gouldsboro' hills on the mainland ; but on the whole there are few roads. There is no turf on which to ride, and the pleasure of keeping horses, except as a convenient means of getting from one place to another, is limited.

But there is always the sea, and to that one comes back with a love that is ever new. Men who know what they are talking about say that Frenchman's Bay is apt to be dangerous for small craft, on account of the sudden squalls which come over the hills and drop on the water like the slap of a tiger's paw, and it would certainly be hard to find a place in which there can be at the same time such an amiable diversity of winds. It is not at all uncommon to see two schooners within a couple of miles of each other, both running close-hauled or both before the wind, but on the same tack and in opposite directions.

Another experience, familiar but always trying, consists in starting with a light but steady southeast breeze which feels as if it would hold through the morning, but which drops out suddenly and completely within half an hour, leaving one bobbing and broiling in a flat calm, until, without warning, it begins to blow hard from some point of the west. Sometimes there is a good sailing breeze at night when the moon is near the full, and to be on the water then is an enchantment. The glistening wake has here and here a shining point of phosphorescence; the familiar lines of the islands are softened with a silver haze; and the whole scene has a certain poetic quality which the positive

beauty of daylight cannot lend to it. One
is reminded of a woman of the world
whom one has known as always sure of
herself and almost hard, until in a moment
of weariness, of weakness, or of sadness, of
fatigue or despondency, the gentler nature
glimmers under the mask.

Entirely apart from the question of ex-
ercise nothing perhaps affords such lasting
amusement at Bar Harbor as rowing, for it
rarely blows so hard that one cannot get
out, and one is independent of calms and
master of one's own time. All along the
shore the granite rocks come down to the
edge of the water, which in many places
lies deep under sheer cliffs. The tide
rises and falls about a dozen feet, and one
may do duller things on a hot morning
than pull slowly, very slowly, along in the
shade at half-tide, watching the starfish
that hold on to the face of the rock with
their red hands, and the brown weed rising
and falling as the water swings slowly back
and forth. If the tide is not too high one
may explore the moderately thrilling re-

cesses of the caves which abound on some of the islands, and if the hour is not too late one may have agreeable converse with some old gentleman who has been visiting his lobster pots, and who has probably sailed every known sea in his time. Of late years several of our ships of war have been at Bar Harbor every summer, and more than once a whole squadron; and the yachts of the New York and Eastern Clubs put in either separately or in little parties. While they are in port the harbor is gay with bunting and laughter and music, and as one sits on the deck of a yacht in the evening the lights of the village, as they go straggling up the hill and along the shore, have a very foreign look, and the cardboard masses of its wooden hotels loom up as if they were really substantial habitations.

After being a few days at Bar Harbor one begins to feel some curiosity about the phases through which it must have passed. There are now a number of cottages, most of them simple, with here and there a few

that are more elaborate, and about a dozen hotels, three or four of which seem to be always full and prosperous, while some others find it at least worth their while to keep open ; but there are still others which have frankly given up the game, and are permanently closed and for sale, though no one seems anxious to buy them. Yet they must have been needed when they were built in the by-gone days, which were not long ago, and after exhausting a friend or two with questions one learns that Bar Harbor already has a past which does not seem likely to repeat itself.

It was discovered nearly thirty years ago by a few artists and students roaming, like Dr. Syntax, in search of the picturesque, and most of them, if they survive, can be moved to rage like the heathen, even at the present day, by reminding them that they could then have bought land for a song by the acre where it now sells by the foot. A few comfort themselves with the reflection that they were only rich in youth and strength in those days, and had no money wherewith to buy land anywhere. Year by year the fame of Bar Harbor spread far and wide, and as one hotel became too crowded another sprang up beside it, until about twelve years ago the place was in the full height of popularity. The few private houses were extremely simple, and nearly everybody lived either in the hotels or in little wooden cottages with no kitchens. The cottagers had to go to one of the hotels for their food, and were known as "mealers" if they were near enough to walk, and "hauled mealers" if they had to be collected with a cart. The little houses are very uncomfortable, and the things to eat at the hotels very bad. Biscuits and preserves formed an appreciable part of the visitor's luggage, and the member of a table who could and would make good salad-dressing became a person of importance, for fresh lobsters and stringy chickens could be bought cheap, and a judicious regular subsidy to the hotel cook was an excellent invest-

ment. If one was asked to dine at a pri- Bar
Harborvate house it was thought better taste not
to boast of it beforehand, nor to talk of it
overmuch afterward, and the host on his
part always expected to provide enough
food to satisfy a crew of famished sailors.
For several seasons men rarely wore evening dress, and such unusual occasions re-
quired previous consultation and discus-
sion, lest one man should seem to be more
formal or ostentatious than the rest. This
was among the quieter "cottage colony,"
but at the large hotels, of which Rodick's
was the most popular, there was little question of sumptuary laws, and at the occasional "hops" young fellows in flannels
and knickerbockers were the partners of
pretty girls gay in the fresh finery which a
woman seems able always to carry in the
most restricted luggage.

The principal characteristic of the place
was an air of youth—it did not seem as if
any one could ever be more than twenty-
five years old. Parties of half a dozen
girls were often under the nominal care of

one chaperon, generally chosen because
she was good natured and not too strict,
but as a matter of fact the young people
protected themselves and one another.
Large picnic parties frequently went off
for the day in buckboards, and there is a
lonely sheet of water among the hills,
called Eagle Lake, which used to be a
favorite goal for afternoon expeditions.
There were canoes and row-boats to be
had, and in the evening supper was ob-
tainable, and better than in the Bar Harbor
hotels, at a little tavern where the prohibi-
tion laws of the State were defied. The
usual result followed, and very bad things
to drink were sold at very high prices, after
paying which the party came home, making the wood-roads ring with laughter and
singing.

That is all changed now. The tavern
is burnt down, a great wooden box in the
lake marks the sluice which takes the village water-supply, people only cross it on
the way to Jordan's Pond, and on moonlight nights it hears but the occasional

splash of a fish, or now and then the wild laughter of the loon. Although parties were popular enough, the pairs who happened to have a temporary affinity were generally in each other's company all day long, wandering over the hills, rowing or paddling on the bay, or sitting on the rocks and islands, each pair out of earshot of the next. On any one of the "Porcupines" there were always sure to be two or three row-boats or canoes drawn up on the little beach; and, as many of their navigators were not used to so high a tide-rise, the skiffs frequently floated off, and it was part of the boatmen's regular business to pick them up and rescue the helpless couples to whom they belonged.

In the evenings when there was moonlight the sight on the bay was really charming. The meal called tea at the hotels tempted no one to linger over it, and as soon as it was over the board-walk was alive with boys and girls hurrying down to the landing-stages, the young man in light flannels, sunburnt and strong, with his companion's bright shawl flung over one shoulder, while the maiden pattered along beside him, her white frock drawn up over a gay striped petticoat, after the fashion of those days, and often her own special paddle in her hand, perhaps with her initials carved carefully thereon and filled in with sealing-wax, rubbed smooth. Then there was a scramble at the floats, and a few minutes later the harbor was covered with boats and canoes, while those who were crowded out consoled themselves by sitting on the rocks along the shore. Slowly each little craft drew away from its neighbor on the quiet water, the young man pulling lazily or wielding the paddle silently with sweeping strokes of his bare brown arm—the girl sitting luxuriously in the stern-sheets, or on a deer-skin in the bottom of the canoe. The sun went down toward Hull's Cove; and as the red glow faded on the upper bay and the moon rose behind Schoodie, twilight merging into moonlight, the rippling note of a girl's laughter or the twang of a banjo rang softly over the water, a white speck showed where a boat was beached on the shingle of an island, while another floated like a black bar into the silver wake of the moon.

Late in the evening the boats came in, one by one, and for those who could afford it there were little supper-parties at Sproul's restaurant, while others contented themselves with mild orgies of biscuits, jam, and the sticky but sustaining caramel. The famous " fish-pond " at Rodick's was a large hall in which the young people used to assemble after breakfast and the early dinner, and in which the girls were supposed to angle for their escorts. It must have been a curious sight. Some of the prettiest girls in all the country were gathered together there, and the soft vowels of the South mingled with the decided con-sonants of the Westerner. As a school of manners the fish-pond had its drawbacks for young men. They were always rather in the minority, and a good-looking college boy was as much run after as a marriage-able British peer, with no ulterior designs, however, on the part of his pursuers, but only the frank determination to "have a good time." People who belonged to the elders even then, and bore the mark of the frump, still tell how startling it was to see a youth sitting on the broad counter of the office and swinging his legs, with his polo cap on the back of his head, while two of the prettiest girls in the world stood and talked to him, in smiling unconsciousness of his rudeness.

Of course such conditions were only possible in a society which still had traditions of a time not very remote, when boys and girls had tramped to and from the village meeting-house and singing-school together, and on the whole it does not seem that any particular harm came of it all. A few imprudent early marriages, a large number of short-lived betrothals, kisses many, and here and there a heartache would sum up the record of a summer at Bar Harbor in the old days. The young men got over their heartaches and married girls whom they would have thought slow

at Mount Desert; the beauty of the board walk married a quiet man who had not been there, and advised her mother not to let her younger sister go, and after a while the newspaper correspondent began to accumulate the stock of stories about summer girls and engagement rings, on which he has been drawing ever since.

The quiet people who liked the climate got tired of living on fried fish and lemon pie, and built themselves houses in chosen spots, with kitchens, and each of them is convinced, and ready to maintain, that he occupies the most thoroughly desirable spot on the island. Fortunately, so far as that is concerned, the wanderer is not called upon to decide where owners disagree, and with happy impartiality he may put away his visit, with all its associations, in the safe cupboard of his pleasant memories.